ISBN 0-86163-630-9 (cased)

Text copyright © Christine Butterworth 1990
Illustrations copyright © Barbara Walker 1990

This edition first published 1993 by
Award Publications Limited,
The Old Riding School, Welbeck Estate,
Nr Worksop, Nottinghamshire

First published 1990 by Hodder and Stoughton
Children's Books

Printed in Singapore
All rights reserved

VEGETABLES

Christine Butterworth

Illustrated by Barbara Walker

AWARD PUBLICATIONS LIMITED

It is a busy Saturday in the market. Vegetables of all shapes and colours are piled high on the stalls.

'What shall we have for lunch?' asks Tom's mum.

All vegetables have vitamins in them which keep you healthy. Vegetables like potatoes, sweet potatoes and yams fill you up and give you energy.

Kamla is shopping in the market, too. Her mother buys potatoes, peas and a shiny purple aubergine. She will cook them with spices to make a spicy Indian vegetable meal.

aubergines   sweet potatoes   yams

Aubergines, sweet potatoes and yams grow in hot places such as Africa and the West Indies.

potatoes   peas

Potatos and peas grow in cooler places in Europe and America.

Vegetables are taken from different parts of plants. Sometimes we eat

the leaves

the flowers

the stem

or

the roots.

Cabbage and lettuce are leaves. Cauliflower and broccoli are flowers. When the flowers die, seeds grow. Sweetcorn and garden peas are the seeds of their plants.

Vegetables such as French beans and okra are the seeds and the pods, too. Celery and leeks are the stems of plants. Carrots, turnips, radishes and beetroots are all roots.

potatoes

Potatoes, yams and sweet potatoes grow underground, but they are not roots. They grow on underground stems, and are called tubers.

yams

sweet potatoes

The salad stall in the market is full of vegetables to eat raw. Tom likes to eat crunchy sticks of raw carrot and cool, juicy cucumber.

Cooked vegetables are softer to eat but cooking kills some of their vitamins.

peppers    celery    carrots

Which of these vegetables would you like to eat raw?

cabbage    chinese leaves    tomatoes

Which ones would you rather eat cooked?

Tom's mum peels the sweet potatoes and boils them in water. Tom likes to eat them mashed, with lots of butter.

Vegetables should not be cooked in too much water, or they lose their goodness. Many vegetables can be steamed over a pan of boiling water.

Kamla and her brother are vegetarians. This means they never eat meat or fish. They eat eggs, nuts and lentils to make sure they keep healthy.

Kamla is a vegetarian because she does not like eating animals. Her grandparents do not eat meat because their religion forbids them to.

Tom's mum keeps her salad vegetables in the fridge so that they stay fresh. Fresh vegetables soon go bad.

Tinned vegetables will keep for months, or even years. In this factory, clean tomatoes are put in cans which are then sealed and heated. Labels are stuck on the cans when they are cool.

Frozen vegetables keep for weeks or months. The peas in this field are picked by a machine called a pea-podder.

The peas are tipped into a lorry which takes them to the factory for freezing. It only takes an hour and a half to get the peas from the plant to the factory freezer.

Most vegetables are grown on farms. The farmer sprays the plants with chemicals to kill weeds and pests which eat the plants.

Some farmers do not spray their crops because they think chemicals harm the soil. The vegetables they grow are called organic. Does your supermarket sell organic vegetables?

You do not always need a lot of space to grow vegetables. You can grow them in a window-box or pot.

Plant some radish seeds in lines, and cover them with a little soil.

Water the soil when it is dry, and wait until the seeds sprout leaves, and grow taller.

After four weeks, you will be able to pull up a radish to eat!

vegetable words

flowers   leaves

pea-podder

roots

salad

stem

tuber